more apples

for a teacher

colleen l. reece & anita corrine donihue

A DayMaker Greeting Book

2

In tribute to teachers

who bring out the best in their students

~with appreciation.

TRAIN A CHILD IN

THE WAY HE SHOULD GO,

AND WHEN HE IS OLD HE

WILL NOT TURN FROM IT.

PROVERBS 22:6 NIV

A time to learn

a teacher's heart

A teacher's heart has many rooms.

Each needs a different key.

Love and caring unbolt some compartments.

Faith and prayer find a way into others.

Patience and compassion pick the locks

of tightly shuttered windows,

letting in the light of hope and encouragement.

Only then can lives be changed, teachers' and students'.

Forever.

A teacher's heart has many rooms.

Each needs a different key,

designed by the Master Teacher

who made the shores of the Sea of Galilee

His classroom and changed the world,

Forever

achievement

Successful teachers are those who have lived well,

laughed often, and loved much;

who have gained the respect of intelligent persons

and the love of children;

who have filled their days and accomplished their tasks;

who leave the world better than they found it . . .

a perfect poem, or a rescued soul;

who never lacked appreciation of earth's beauty

or failed to express it;

who looked for the best in others

and gave the best they had.

ADAPTED FROM
ROBERT LOUIS STEVENSON

inner vison

If you could see beneath the rumpled hair,

The pizza-stained shirt, behind the freckles.

If you could look inside a squirming body,

Dreamy eyes staring out the window,

What would you find?

A second Einstein? Another Michelangelo?

Or a child like every other child,

Longing for you to turn the key,

To set him free to become what he longs to be.

bless the teachers

Lord, please bless all teachers.

You have given them the responsibility

of training those who must grasp the future.

May it not be with uncertain hands,

but with confidence.

May those You have called to point the way

first learn it from Thee.

children of
the heavenly father

Children of the heavenly Father

Safely in His bosom gather;

Nestling bird nor star in heaven

Such a refuge e'er was given.

Though He giveth or He taketh,

God His children ne'er forsaketh,

His the loving purpose solely

To preserve them pure and holy.

CAROLINE V. SANDELL BERG, 1855

It takes a special kind of love,

the patience of Job,

and the wisdom of Solomon

to parent, teach, and minister

to children with special needs.

Yet even small triumphs bring great joy

and affirm that such efforts are worthwhile.

And whoever welcomes a little child like this

in my name welcomes me.

MATTHEW 18:5 NIV

If you can bring

one moment of

happiness into the life

of a child, you are

a coworker with God.

Encourager

The first time I met seven-year-old Lacey, she stole my heart. Her long, blond ponytail bounced behind her, reflecting her bubbly personality. Her blue eyes sparkled from behind thick, heavy glasses. And I soon learned that her sparsely-toothed grin is a smile that doesn't quit.

Lacey has Down's Syndrome. In spite of her difficulty in learning quickly, she is curious and eager to try. She ran so fast during recess I could barely keep up. Everyone marveled at the way she performed flips and turns on the monkey bars. Friends from all classes flocked to her. Sometimes Lacey was overwhelmed and covered her eyes until I helped her escape from so much excitement. Before she did, she always hugged the other students, whom she genuinely loved.

Unlike the other kids, Lacey never called me Mrs. Donihue or Mrs. D., she's always called me "Teach." At times she could be stubborn. Arms and legs crossed on the rug, she would refuse to do her work, but her pout would soon leave and her irresistible smile return.

After three years with us, Lacey moved on to another school. I could barely contain the tears when we said good-bye. We had developed a special kind of love.

Lacey still has a corner of my heart. I keep her picture up and pray for her. Occasionally, she returns to visit our class. And one of my biggest thrills is when I'm in a store or restaurant and hear her unmistakable strong, husky voice call, "Hey, Teach!" The world around us seems to stop. Lacey dashes toward me and I brace myself. Arms and legs fly around my waist and neck in a vise-like hug that I joyfully return. Then I hear the words that warm and melt my heart. "I love you, Teach. I love you special."

following stars

Ralph Waldo Emerson said, "Hitch your wagon to a star." The three wise men probably had no wagon, but they followed the Star of the East. It led them to the world's greatest treasure, Jesus, lying in a manger near Bethlehem. And surely God smiles when dedicated teachers encourage their students to follow their own particular stars.

I am here for a purpose.
I came from heaven above
With something great to give you:
A special kind of love.

did they know?

Did the disciples know as they
sat at Jesus' feet and learned
life's most important lessons, that
one day they would pick up the
torch of His teachings and carry
light into a dark world?
What teachers instill in young
minds is the spark from which
generations of flaming torches
of truth may be lit.

EVERY MAN'S LIFE

IS A FAIRY-TALE

WRITTEN BY

GOD'S FINGERS.

HANS CHRISTIAN
ANDERSEN

Heart and soul

At six weeks of age, she became ill. Doctors seriously and tragically erred in her treatment. As a result, she lost her eyesight and could only distinguish darkness from light.

In spite of her disability, her parents and teachers encouraged her to try as many things as possible during childhood. She loved to climb trees and ride horses bareback. Remarkably, she memorized huge portions of the Bible. Later, she studied at the Northwest Institute for the Blind, then remained at the school to teach history and language.

She weighed no more than a hundred pounds as a young lady. Not attractive by conventional standards, her wit, grace, and charm captured listeners when she spoke. Her compassion for the needy, for street people, and for children made her lovely in heart and spirit. Her music and poetry filled our world. She wrote between eight thousand and nine thousands hymns and at seventy-one, penned one of her best-loved hymns, "Saved by Grace." Her name was Fanny Crosby.

*H*ans Christian Andersen was the son of a poor shoe-maker in Denmark who died when Hans was eleven years old. He attended the Odense city school for poor children. Later a friend helped him get a scholarship to continue his education.

Was it there he first began to write? To observe life and weave moral teachings into his fairy-tales, plays, and novels? Perhaps. Who can forget the excitement when first hearing how *The Ugly Duckling* (based on Andersen's own life) became a glorious swan? Or how Hans poked fun at persons who thought too highly of themselves by penning *The Emperor's New Clothes?*

Generations of adults and children continue to enjoy and learn from Hans Christian Andersen's work.

pebble on the shore

I do not know what I may appear to the world,

but to myself I seem to have been only

like a boy playing on the seashore,

and diverting myself in now and then

finding a smoother pebble or a pretty shell,

whilst the great ocean of truth lay

all undiscovered before me.

SIR ISAAC NEWTON

Yesterday is only a memory,

tomorrow a hope.

Today is ours.

Be prepared in season and out of season. . . .
2 TIMOTHY 4:2 NIV

In all these things we are

more than conquerors

through him who loved us.
ROMANS 8:37 NIV

IF THERE BE WORDS OF

KINDNESS OR ENCOURAGEMENT,

SPEAK THEM NOW.

SOMEONE, SOMEWHERE,

IS WAITING FOR THEM.

Opportunity

A teacher once thought she would write and congratulate a coworker on a special achievement. Instead, she grew busy and failed to do so. She excused herself by saying her letter would never be missed in the wealth of congratulations the other teacher would be sure to receive.

Some time later, she met her fellow instructor and apologized. To her amazement and dismay, the hardworking teacher had not received even one congratulatory note of commendation or appreciation.

John Ruskin once said two sad things happen when we fail to praise. We run the risk of driving a person from the right road for want of encouragement, and we deprive ourselves of the happy privilege of rewarding deserving labor.

Lord, may we always be quick to praise, slow to criticize.

The man without purpose is like a ship

without a rudder — a waif, a nothing, a no man.

Have a purpose in life, and having it,

throw such strength of mind and muscle

into your work as God has given you.

27

Thomas Carlyle certainly knew adversity. He experienced one of the worst things that can happen to an author. After completing the first volume of his book, *The French Revolution*, his friend John Stuart Mill borrowed the manuscript. By accident, Mill's housemaid burned the manuscript! Carlyle didn't give up, however. He rewrote the book, largely from memory. It was finally published in 1837.

If the computer eats your lesson plans, remember Thomas Carlyle!

The first Sunday my husband and I visited our new church, we were made to feel welcome, but something was missing. The tiny congregation, made up mostly of older people, had no children. We knew God had led us to this church. It was plain to see we were needed. Everyone longed to hear the sound of children's laughter echo through the building.

What could I do to help? I already taught school during the week and worked nights at a second job. Still, I felt God's tugging. Could He be leading me to teach the children we hoped would come? Where would I find the physical strength? Most of all, where would the kids come from?

A young mother and her two-year-old daughter Sierra began attending church. Dark, tightly-curled ringlets framed the little girl's warm brown eyes and irresistible smile. I fell hopelessly in love with Sierra. Each time I turned around, she had her arms outstretched, waiting for me to pick her up.

God, there is only this one child, I prayed. *Can we reach more? Please help us multiply into many children.*

The following spring a vision for a Vacation Bible School struck me. And I knew I was the only one who could direct it. And though it was summer vacation, with my second job I would still have to function on four to five hours of sleep each night if I directed the week-long VBS. I prayed for strength and we launched into the program. Some said we couldn't do it, but our church's grandmas and grandpas showed up in force to go door knocking, then mustered their energy and skills and did what was needed. Kids came. We were successful. At the end of the week, we had a church school promotional picnic.

Next came the question: Who would teach the Primary/Junior class? We didn't even have teaching materials. Feeling nudged, I committed to six months. I dug remnants of teaching materials out of storage and poured my heart into the program. Before long we averaged fifteen to twenty kids each week. Less than a year later, I watched six eager Juniors and one older brother tell of their love for God and be baptized. I was so happy I cried and thanked God.

Now the once-quiet halls of our church ring with children's laughter after worship. And when I feel that familiar tug at my skirt, I gather little Sierra into my arms. I can hardly wait for the day she is old enough to join my class, for I will continue teaching. With God's help, not only the children, but my commitment to love and teach has multiplied.

honor bound

I am not bound to win,

but I am bound to be true.

I am not bound to succeed,

but I am bound to live

by the light that I have.

I must stand with anybody

that stands right,

stand with him while he is right,

and part [company] with him

when he goes wrong.

ABRAHAM LINCOLN

*E*ight-year-old Anthony watched the kids play kickball. Anthony cheered and clapped his hands. Each time there was a catch, kick, or home run, he strained at his wheelchair seat belt, clapping and kicking with excitement. How he longed to be in that game!

Then it happened. The ball landed smack in Anthony's lap. He grabbed it with both hands. His brown eyes glowed and a bright smile lit up his face. Although he couldn't speak, Anthony showed what he could do. With a mighty heave, he sailed the ball across the diamond to home base!

The other kids were shocked, then excited. They all cheered wildly. Everyone knew Anthony loved ball games. He went to pro baseball games with his family and watched every game he could on TV. But what the kids didn't know was that Anthony and his dad spent many hours together playing catch in the park and in the family's backyard.

Soon Anthony was made pitcher. He not only pitched well, he put several people out. When his turn came to kick, one of the other kids helped him. Then Anthony flew from base to base in his wheelchair while his team cheered him on.

Even though the game went a little slower, everyone—especially Anthony—had more fun and all showed good team spirit. If you ask, you'll find that Anthony and his team are always ready for another game.

> There never shall be one lost good.
> All we have willed or hoped
> or dreamed of good shall exist.
> ROBERT BROWNING

LORD, HELP US

TO ALWAYS SHOW

APPRECIATION TO THOSE

AROUND US

In good hands

Albrecht Durer longed to draw and paint, but he came from a poor family in Germany. His older friend also wanted to become a great artist and suggested they live together. They struggled to earn enough to put food on the table, so Durer's friend said, "I will make our living. When your paintings begin to sell, I will have my chance." He waved away Durer's protests. "I have a job in a restaurant. I am also older and have not so much talent. You must not waste your years." The friend worked long hours, planning for the wonderful day he would be free to pursue his goal.

Albrecht studied hard. At last he sold a wood carving. "Now I shall be the breadwinner," he declared. "Go to your paints, my friend."

The older man took up his brush. Alas for his dreams. Years of hard work had twisted his hands. He could no longer hold the brush with mastery and skill. Albrecht Durer found his friend in prayer, hands clasped. Durer could not give back the lost skill, but his wonderful painting "The Praying Hands" captures the spirit of a noble, unselfish man who sacrificed his dreams to help another.

Work first, then rest.

JOHN RUSKIN

38

*E*very week James delivered his son to church school, drove home, picked up his wife, and returned in time for eleven o'clock service. One sunny morning when they pulled up in front of the church, young Jimmy crossed his arms, stuck out his lower lip, and announced, "I ain't going."

"Of course you are," James exclaimed. "Go on, son." Jimmy shook his head violently and stuck his lip out farther. "Naw. If it ain't good enough for you, it ain't good enough for me."

The next week, the whole family attended church school. Actions really do speak louder than words.

looking up

Far away there in the sunshine

are my highest aspirations.

I may not reach them,

but I can look up and see their beauty,

believe in them,

and try to follow where they lead.

LOUISA MAY ALCOTT

39

Genius is undiscovered gold.

Talented is the teacher

who struggles, finds,

and helps students develop it.

*W*hat were they like, those who taught Jesus?

Did Joseph teach Him songs, psalms, and passages from the Torah? Did he teach lessons traditionally passed from father to son? Did he place tiny Jesus on a stool to learn the carpenter trade? Or give Him livelihood skills? Surely he exhibited unfaltering faith in the One true God, strength to love and protect Jesus by God's directions.

What about Mary? Did she share with Jesus what God had revealed to her, or hold her secrets within, letting the boy discover His own answers from God? Perhaps she showed Him nature's miracles and taught Him to respect the beauty, dangers, and frailty in plants and animals. Did His mother model gentleness, love, responsibility? Did she teach Jesus geography while balancing Him on her hip, naming the Plain of Esdraelon, the Jordan valley? Did His keen gaze follow her pointing finger across the valley to Mount Carmel, or the closer Mt. Tabor?

How did she describe the waves, the breeze, the many storms on the Sea of Galilee? Did Jesus see His mother frown when she spoke of sharp pyramids and the Sphinx? Her eyes would have sparkled when she painted word pictures of the Mount of Olives, Jerusalem, and of the beloved temple. Her longing to return to the sacred place of worship must have been contagious.

As Jesus grew, did His mother ever correct Him? In learning to obey her and Joseph, Jesus surely learned unquestioning obedience to His heavenly Father.

Who were His grandparents? Was Jesus close to them? Did they instill priceless wisdom, exhibiting by their lives a zest for life Jesus could mirror? Perhaps they taught Him patience and the ability to speak out for truth and righteousness. His teachers in the synagogue may have been kind and caring, or stern and aloof. Either way, the rabbis must have opened to

Jesus the mysteries in God's Word, by insisting on perfection from the Christ Child as He memorized passage after passage. When He challenged their teachings, they had no idea He was the Son of God—although they marveled at His perception. If they had accepted Jesus' challenges, they would have poured their entire knowledge into Him, heart and soul, seeing light and hope for the future even in One so young.

What did the shepherds teach Jesus? Did He see how they were willing to lay down their lives for their sheep? Were they unknowingly preparing Him to someday become the Good Shepherd? Journeying to Jerusalem for the Passover as a twelve-year-old reinforced Jesus' lessons in history and geography. Storytellers among His fellow travelers undoubtedly predicted the coming of the Messiah.

Did His Aunt Elisabeth teach Jesus? Did she share any secrets she had learned twelve years before? Or did she, too, keep silent? What if the family could have seen beyond the meager sacrifice of the roasted Paschal lamb and seen the true Lamb of God?

What was the high priest in the temple like? Did the promise he and the wise elders discerned in Jesus make them feel threatened, without knowing why?

What did Jesus learn from His heavenly Father, in early-morning solitude and prayer? We cannot know if or when the Author and Finisher, Teacher above all teachers, laid the eternal plan of salvation before the boy-man Jesus, step by painful step. Did God expect His Son to unconditionally obey? Did He reveal to Jesus how the supreme sacrifice would explode in holy triumph, victory, and eternal life for all who believed and accepted? Did even one of Jesus' earthly teachers suspect who they taught? Were any, other than God, worthy to guide His only Son?

GOODNESS

IS THE ONLY

INVESTMENT

THAT NEVER FAILS.

HENRY DAVID THOREAU

Someone cared

The story is told of a doctor in Wales who was called to care for a desperately ill child on a terrible night. Devotion to duty and love for God's children forced him to brave one of the worst storms the countryside had ever seen and respond to the call. Years later, the child he saved rose to high places. Many times the old doctor shook his head and marveled. There had been no way for him to know the far-reaching effects of his actions. He had faced the wild storm to care for the child of a widowed mother, a child he believed would become a common laborer.

In so doing, the doctor actually saved the life of a future Prime Minister.

prayer for a teacher

Lord, please bless all teachers.

Those who serve in public schools,

in private schools, in homeschools.

And those who teach Your Word

in church school classes.

Each have chosen paths for which they are best suited;

paths that will best serve their students.

Guide their feet that they may not stumble or lose the way,

lest those following after lose sight of the goal

and settle for little knowledge

when much is needed.

work unseen

A teacher built a temple,
wrought with skill and care,
Formed each pillar with patience,
Layed each stone with prayer.
None saw the unceasing effort,
None knew of the marvelous plan,
For the temple the teacher built
Was unseen by the eyes of man.

ADAPTED,
AUTHOR UNKNOWN

Kelly stood near nine-year-old Manuel's wheelchair during noon recess. Only a week of school remained, so all the classroom balls and other playground equipment were checked in.

Kelly's students wondered what they could do.

"Why don't you run races to the fence (a distance of about two blocks) and back?" she suggested. "Get ready. Get set. Go!" Off ran a half dozen kids.

Manuel watched longingly. He couldn't walk or speak, though he signed a little. Now he motioned for his teacher to help him out of his chair and onto the grass. Several of Manuel's good fifth-grade friends joined him. Manual looked as though he desperately wanted to race with the other kids. He glanced up at Kelly and they exchanged smiles.

Julie, a mother helper, happened along just then. "He wants to be in the race more than anything," Kelly told Julie. A few minutes later, Kelly said, "Well, look at that! He's going to give it a try." She felt surprised and thrilled. Manuel crawled about six feet across the grass and turned for her approval. Kelly nodded and gave him a big smile. Soon his fifth-grade friends joined him. "I can't believe it," Kelly exclaimed. "They're pacing him!"

Manuel reached the halfway point. Kelly glanced at her watch and turned to Julie. "Will you please get Manuel while I gather the other kids?" Julie started across the play yard. The look on Manuel's face showed pure determination.

I don't care if we're late getting in, Kelly decided. *This is more important.* She motioned the group on. More kids entered the race, walking at Manuel's speed.

They finally reached the fence. Manuel turned and started back. Sometimes he flopped on the grass. The others flopped with him. Then he was on his way again. Soon all his friends were on their knees crawling along with him. Julie walked at Manuel's side. Kelly and other students cheered when he approached the finish line back where he had started. He grinned as though he had completed a marathon. His brown eyes snapped with excitement.

Kelly bent down and helped him step carefully to his chair. His little legs trembled. "Manuel, I'm so proud of you!" She gathered his small body in her arms and placed him in his chair while everyone clapped.

Manuel looked proud and thrilled. He'd finished the race and knew he'd won!

Love conquers all things;
let us too surrender to love.
VIRGIL

Teach me, then, Lord,

to bring to

all that I may be,

To all I do,

my God and King,

A consciousness of thee.

George Herbert

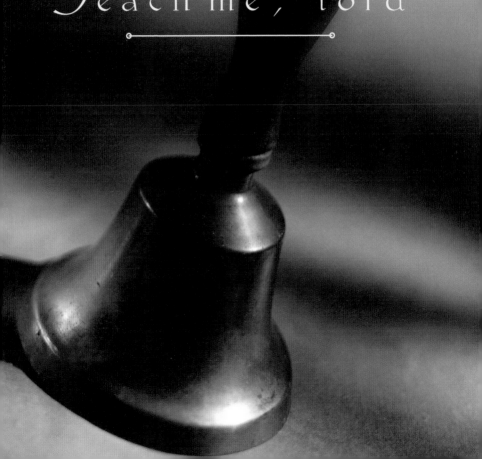

Teach me, lord

who am I?

Who am I, Lord, to teach children?

There is so much I do not know.

How can I teach the importance of loving?

I struggle so.

Lord, may my students always see

The real teaching come from Thee.

MOTTO ON A SUN DIAL.

"I only mark the hours that shine."

© 2003 by Barbour Publishing, Inc.

ISBN 1-58660-699-9

Cover images ©Ann Cutting/Photonica
Book design by Kevin Keller| designconcepts

Published by Barbour Books, an imprint of Barbour Publishing, Inc.,
P.O. Box 719, Uhrichsville, Ohio 44683, www.barbourbooks.com

Member of the
Evangelical Christian
Publishers Association

Printed in China.

5 4 3 2 1